GO FOR THE GOAL

GO FOR THE GOAL

Fifty-two corner kicks of
ANDREW KUYVENHOVEN

Designed and illustrated by
MARGARET HOFLAND

BOARD OF PUBLICATIONS OF THE CHRISTIAN REFORMED CHURCH

Credit: Jack Harkema, page 12

Library of Congress Cataloging in Publication Data

Kuyvenhoven, Andrew.
  Go for the goal.

  Originally appeared in the Banner.
  1. Meditations.   I. Banner (Grand Rapids, Mich.)
II. Title.
BV4832.2.K85   1984   242   84-12467

ISBN 0-930265-00-9

To Ena, wife and mother.

CONTENTS

Introduction   13
Prophet and Ape   15
Three Classrooms   16
Child Teaches Parents   18
Parental Love   21
Kids Need Moms and Dads   22
Sleepless Nights   24
Clothing   26
Forgiven Sinners   28
The Best Photo   30
The Gift of Faith   33

Spiritual Butterflies 34
Mailbox 36
Sex and Cold Potatoes 38
Vows and Feelings 40
To Catch a Thief 42
Florida 44
Mother's Day 46
Lost Sheep 48
Evangelical Handbook on Eating 50
Too Much Organ 52
Snoopervision 54
The Crack in the Concrete 58
God and the Salmon 60
Fight Sin and Ignorance 62
Teenagers 64
No Retakes 66
It's Easier the Second Time 68
Music in China 70
Statistical Evidence 72
Praying Together 74
Holy Forgetfulness 76
Easter Comes in Spring 78
We Need Grandparents 80
More of the Same 82
Heaven or Hell 84
Devil in Church 86
Out of Step 88
Fearful or Firm? 90
Outrage 93

To Uphold and to Govern   94
No Greeting Time   96
Camping   98
Communication   101
Windows in Heaven   102
Heatwave   106
Living with Pain   108
Argue, You Lose   110
This Rhythm or that Rut   113
Total Depravity   114
Why?   117
Past Tense Is Forever   118
The Final Answer   120

Since September 1980 I have written a weekly column entitled "Corner Kick" in *The Banner*, the weekly magazine of the Christian Reformed Church.

Most readers—but not all of them—know that a corner kick is a penalty in soccer. A free kick is awarded to the attackers when a member of the defending team steers the ball over the end-line on either side of the goal. A player of the attacking team kicks the ball from the corner at the right or the left side of the defenders' goal line. If the ball is well aimed, it sails in a gracious arch towards the goal mouth. The attacking players try to head or kick the ball into the goal. If they do, they score.

I chose Corner Kick as the name of the weekly column for a number of good reasons. The best reason, I thought, was that a corner kick presents an opportunity to score, although I know very well that not *every* corner kick results in a goal.

The purpose of *The Banner* and of my writing is that all of us reach the goal. We must become the kind of people God wants us to be.

Compared with a sermon, a Corner Kick is an indirect attempt to make my teammates go for the goal.

My wife, my daughter, and the Board of Publications thought that this particular selection of Corner Kicks could help many to live goal-oriented lives. I hope they are right.

The Germans have a saying: "It is with books as it is with mirrors: when an ape looks into it, you cannot expect a prophet to look out of it."

I have been pondering how I could most effectively use that famous saying.

I thought I might keep it for one of my worst critics. If he writes me a letter saying that he can find no good in our magazine, I might write to him: "Dear Sir, It is with *The Banner* as it is with mirrors: when an ape looks into it, you cannot expect a prophet to look out of it. Sincerely, The Editor."

But that would be unfair. Some of our critics are our best friends.

Come to think of it, the whole saying is very defensive and liable to be abused by any arrogant author or artist.

I have been at art exhibitions where some paintings seemed to me duller than most wallpaper, and other canvasses were more smeared and smudgy than the old pants I wear for work around the house. Even if all the patrons of the arts tell me that the price is a hundred thousand dollars because a prophet is eyeing me from that canvas, I am not going to be bowled over. I'll say that it is an ape or, maybe, a baby prophet.

Same thing with books. If you believe the blurbs on the covers, there are wells of wisdom, flashes of insight, and masterful mysteries in all of them. Prophets are looking out of them, say the publishers. As a matter of fact there are many apes, naked apes, writing books.

Of course there is truth in the saying. As a matter of fact, the saying is in agreement with a word from the Bible: only those who receive a prophet as a prophet will receive the true reward. A dull person (the "ape") cannot discern the voice of prophecy.

So, the only book on which one could write the saying about the prophet and the ape is The Book. Unless the reader has the Spirit of the prophets, she or he will never discern the true message of the Bible.

15

THREE CLASSROOMS

I have nearly passed through the three stages of my education: first, my parents raised me; then, my wife taught me; next, my children educated me. This last phase is not quite finished.

All things considered, my parents did a good job. Of course, they had certain advantages none of my other teachers had. They put things into me I did not know I had received until twenty years later. I have forgotten all their lectures about God and life and duty (if ever they gave such lectures), yet I find their teachings in my bones and marrow. When I am confronted with certain ideas, events, or persons, feelings well up from the depth of my subconscious. And, when I have put those feelings into words, I hear my father talking.

When I meet my brother, who is now a middle-aged man, I notice that he holds his head the way my father used to hold his. I don't do that, of course. I hold my own head in my own way. At least, that's what I like to think.

Then came my wife. When you get married, you have no idea what you're in for. That's why it's a good thing most of us marry when we're young and somewhat reckless. Otherwise, we'd lack the courage forever.

I am sure she did not set out to change me. She did not have a hidden agenda. I would have discovered and exposed it. She taught me and changed me, but it's hard to admit that she did it, and harder still to explain *how* she did it. Somehow a wife gets her fingers onto the switch of your heart. I suppose it works both ways, but I'm scared to say it out loud. She might put hers on "off."

The children aren't through with me yet. Today, I have neither the audacity, nor the space, to tell you what they have already taught me. I'll spend another week in their school and report to you later.

16

CHILD TEACHES PARENTS

We must now think of that department of the school of life in which our children are our teachers.

When the marriage brings the child—rather than the child the marriage—the arrival of the first one is a big surprise from God. She was that to me. I did contemplate, during courtship, what marital bliss I was about to receive. But being a father was no part of my fantasy. Even if you have as many smaller brothers and sisters as I had, it does not at all prepare you for being a parent. Having your own child is another dimension of life, a second story of happiness, a place you cannot reach until you have climbed the stairway.

Maybe you think I am exaggerating. Knowing my own weakness in storytelling, I would be inclined to think so myself. But I have relived the experience so often by observing others, that I am now positive in my theory about the shock treatment in our educational process that happens when a baby makes us parents.

I have deeply involved myself in the lives of young boys who were the sons of the congregations I served. I won't talk about the daughters now, just the sons. By "deeply involved" I mean that I watched them when they sat in church. I taught them in catechism, I prayed with them and for them, and I heard their confessions of faith. I worried about them. Less than their parents, of course, but I worried nevertheless. They can do such stupid things. Cars and money and girls and beer and summer nights, any and all can send a spark to their combustion chamber: Boom! But okay, most of them get a "good girl." They marry, I talk to them, I preach to them, and they drive off with the paper roses on the car.

Then comes the big change. One day he calls me on the phone. It's either very early in the morning or very late at night. When you hear his voice, you drop what you are doing or thinking. Listen to his voice. It has a new timbre. The mystery has happened. "It's a boy (girl)," he says. "Yes, Beth is fine, I mean, she's. . .ah. . .terrific." "Then I guess you and I will be thanking God tonight." "I did already," he says.

When you go to him and her to discuss the baptism, you are talking to a *man*. He experiences a responsibility he never felt before. And he loves it.

Then they show you seven and a half pounds of humanity through with God performed an educational miracle.

Parental love is the kind of love that is ready to make sacrifices. Before you are a parent, you cannot imagine yourself getting up in the middle of the night to change a diaper or to warm a bottle. But God has arranged life in such a way that self-centered beings can learn to forget about themselves when they have to care for their children. And it comes easy. You don't have to be superspiritual to make all sorts of sacrifices for your children. Animals lick their young, defend them, play with them, teach them. And any normal human being does the same, except for the licking.

A teenager cannot imagine that some late evening he or she will stay up to wait for his or her teenager to come home. The parent will be sitting there, steaming behind the darkened window. Slowly the anger will melt for the fear that something has happened. Now the parent is praying for the sound of the car, the noise of the barking muffler, which, at this time of night, would be sweeter than any symphony. But when the car turns into the driveway, fear departs and anger returns.

And so we learn. They who have children gather joy and pain, never the one without the other.

To parents God gives the ability to forgive more than seven times. Children may step on your heart, but you'll forgive them. They may waste money in riotous living, disobey your orders, but the moment they return to your town on the Greyhound bus, with long hair but short of everything else, you press them to your chest and forgive all.

The Giver of life is the Teacher of love. In parenthood he teaches us a special dimension of love. The children do not have to feel guilty that we have loved them when they hurt us. Neither should they ever think that they must repay the love of their parents. That's not the way God put life together. You can never love your parents in the same way they loved you. You give that kind of love to your children, when God gives you your turn.

KIDS NEED MOMS AND DADS

Nowadays many couples get married but they don't have children for a long time. That's not my business, of course. It's theirs. I know of a minister in Canada who went to admonish a childless couple, saying that if there were no medical reasons that prevented the birth of a child, they "ought to do their duty according to Genesis 1:28." The young husband was furious. He did not put up a theological argument; he said "Get out!" and "You aren't the priest."

I must confess that my wife and I have often said to each other how nice it might have been if she and I would have spent the first years of our marriage going to school together, working in turn to support each other. But at that time we never discussed it. We did not even think of it.

Actually I am happy that, in those days, the question did not come up. At least in that respect life was simple. Whenever I feel inclined to be envious of the young, who have all sorts of opportunities we never had, I also feel an edge of sadness. They have to answer so many more questions and make so many more decisions. Life is more difficult for them. It is very human to give the wrong answer to a question, and it is very painful to make the wrong decision. We pray often for renewed mercies and fresh wisdom so that young people may find the right answers in a new age.

There's just one thing I want to bind on the hearts of those who are young parents, if I could. As long as you have young children, you must be, first and last, parents.

As long as you have someone slamming the screen door and shouting, "Mom, I'm home," mom or dad ought to be there. Those are moments of eternal significance, believe it or not. If there are not parents then and there, if there are only two quarters on the kitchen counter and the message to get a drink and a donut, you are sowing the wind, and you will tremble when the harvest comes.

Let me talk to all those who have children under fourteen: right now you are their heroes and their sunshine. As yet your smile makes them happy, your frown makes them cry. Your home is their castle, their best spot on earth, no matter what it looks like to you or your neighbors. As yet they are running to you. If you fail them now, you'll never be able to make up.

SLEEPLESS NIGHTS

For about fifty years I have received good nights of refreshing sleep, night after night. Yes, thank you. And praise the Lord. It's his gift to his beloved, says Psalm 127:2.

After hanging my clothes on the bedroom chair, leaving my socks on the floor, and laying my worries before the throne of God, I have nearly always surrendered to a deep sleep.

I don't think that the Lord loves me less than last night, but sleep does not come. So, I get out of bed, I make a pot of tea, and I eat some crackers.

Of course, I know the reasons: too much mental activity and too little physical activity. The wheels keep on turning.

I have now read Matthew 6 and I am still not sleepy.

Recently I read somewhere the number of sleeping pills ·North America eats. I cannot remember big figures. I must always check a book to see how many miles the moon is distant from the earth, although I've heard it a hundred times. And the number of pills exceeds that number of miles.

Perhaps I should speak more kindly of those who take a pill. And maybe I should pray for those who are tempted to drink liquor when they cannot sleep.

Anyway, we should not act as if life is coming apart when we cannot sleep. Why don't I enjoy the quietude of these moments? I don't because I fear that I will not be able to function well tomorrow.

I know at least two people, and one of them is my brother, who read *The Banner* when they cannot sleep. But I hate to think that it works better than a sleeping pill.

Actually, they did not tell me that they read *The Banner* during sleepless nights because it makes them sleepy. They meant to say that sleepless nights enabled them to do what they could not get done during the day. Yes, of course, that's it: sleepless nights give people a second chance to do what they could not get done.

This night it seems to me that more prayers are said by Christians during sleepless nights than at any other time. I think that the number of prayers offered during sleepless nights is greater than the amount of miles the moon is distant from the earth.

I'll have one more cup of tea. And a cracker.

CLOTHING   Do not be anxious, said the Lord Jesus, when you ask yourself the question "Wherewithal shall we be clothed?"

We suffer from the anxiety of choice, not of scarcity.

Here is a woman staring at her wardrobe with disgust in her eyes. Impatiently she pushes the hangers over the metal rod in her closet. And she cries out: "Wherewithal shall I be clothed?"

There is a man, a respectable man, ready to retire in his chamber. He says: "I cannot wear that jacket tomorrow because I wore it yesterday."

And yonder is a high school student, going through the drawer for the third time, desperately looking for the pair of jeans that would be right.

"Wherewithal shall we be clothed?" The question is packed with emotion, filled with anxiety, and thrust upon us by a hidden tyrant.

Freedom from one master is usually found by surrender to another. When millions of Chinese people kowtowed to their former government, they denied the gods of shirts and ties and dresses. While Mr. Nixon was president of the USA, all of us got a peep through the bamboo curtain, and we saw a million drab blue ants in the uniform of the revolution.

Ever since that time I have been playing with the idea of a Christian uniform. What would happen if all Christians agreed to wear a simple dress for $39.95 or a pair of overalls for $29.50? Think of it! All competition would be finished. This would be the wherewithal for every high school class and for every worship service. Megatons of energy would come free for more useful service. And all of us would laughingly admit the folly of our former slavery.

Recently, on TV, I saw a Chinese woman on a bicycle. She wore a colorful garment, and she had a packaged TV set on the carrier. I knew that this was the clearest sign that the wave of the old revolution had spent itself and that China was ready to serve another tyrant, a cruel gang of four: Vogue, Couture, Fad and Fashion.

26   We don't want to be slaves. We are called to be free. But it is hard

to be free from anxiety—the kind of anxiety that goes with scarcity as well as the anxiety that comes with abundance.

It's an insult to think that God loves only drabness of sackcloth or blackness of sobriety. But it's equally silly to think that the Lord is impressed by all the glory of Solomon and contemporary fashion.

Somehow it is entirely correct that in the hospital all patients are robed in formless gowns and all of the staff is dressed in uniforms. After all, this is one place where everybody knows that the body is more than raiment.

FORGIVEN SINNERS

On Thanksgiving Day and on a few other occasions we used to have each of the children mention one thing for which they were thankful to God. They would mention health, sunshine, and report cards that turned out better than expected. Sometimes they would even say: "I thank God for loving parents" or "for a Christian home."

28

Once, when we were going through this thanksgiving list, one of the younger ones said: "I thank God for the forgiveness of my sins."

That took us by surprise. The other children were grinning, thinking that their little sister could not think of something else to be grateful for. And we, parents, had a fleeting thought that our little daughter might have a big sin we did not know about.

I don't like it when children talk about sin too much and too generally. My wife and I noticed that when our children came to third and fourth grades—when they had learned praying aloud in Christian school, they would always say, near the end, "and forgive us our many sins, forJesus'sakeamen." I try not to criticize a prayer, because prayers go to God. But you do wonder if all these fourth graders who say "forgive our many sins, forJesus'sakeamen" could mention a couple of their sins by name.

Nevertheless, I want to testify today that I am deeply thankful for the forgiveness of my sins.

I have learned that I do not know God, I do not know self, and I do not know what gratitude is unless I know thankfulness for the forgiveness of my sins.

An older minister once told how he had a young girl in his congregation who had a "terminal disease." She had been in bed at her parents' home for half a year. He loved the weekly visits, especially because her father was the kind of man who really knew how to talk about subjects that interest a preacher: other preachers and their shortcomings.

At one such visit, when he had been talking to the father about covenantal and expository preaching, my older friend turned to go and said to the girl, "Well, Robin, shall we pray together?"

"May I ask something?" said the girl. "But, of course . . ." said the preacher. And Robin said: "Sir, are there preachers also in heaven?"

At first he was dumbfounded. Then my preacher friend choked up. Finally he said: "No, Robin, there aren't any preachers in heaven. In heaven there are only forgiven sinners."

THE BEST PHOTO

I am the second worst photographer. When I was given a camera—there have been those birthdays—the loving givers assured me that this was the kind of camera that eliminated all flops. "Just press the button." But I always managed to do what the advertisements say nobody could do.

The worst photographer is a somewhat older friend of mine whose name I'll never tell. He was given a camera by his grownup children when he and his wife went on their first real trip. He took lots of pictures and the whole family got together to see the slides on a special evening. There were two strange things about the pictures: first, the photographer could not recognize any of the scenes that appeared on the screen in the darkened room. Second, every one of the pictures had a sort of dark visor at the side, as if the father had been covering part of the lens with his thumb. Finally, one of his smart children put it all together: Dad had been using the camera backwards, shooting every picture over his shoulder. Therefore the scenery was never what he had been looking at, and his ear was in every one of the pictures.

I do have one priceless picture. I took it when we lived in Lethbridge on the day when I brought my wife home with our fifth child. Straight from the hospital we went to the bedroom. There the baby was put into the cradle and all four of our children crowded around.

The picture is of the cradle. You cannot see the baby. But the four children are all vibrant attention: necks are craned, bodies stretched. If one would try to arrange for such a shot, I'm sure it would take hours of posing. This one came spontaneously. Every one of the four is simply and totally interested in the new baby. Their little bodies are tense with eagerness, happiness, love, reception.

While I'm sitting here, looking at that picture, the imaginary photographer in me is vanishing and the seer takes charge. Now I see all sorts of people: Indians of the U.S. and Canada, some wooden shoe people, Chinese, Koreans, Scotch, and lots of Hispanic people. All of them stand around a cradle. They are craning their necks, and their bodies are stretched with attention, eyes hungry with love.

Now I see the most majestic photograph anybody ever shot: Jesus in a cradle and the whole world is stretching, grasping, hoping. All attention is riveted on one Baby. And they cry to each other: Look! Behold! Unto us a Child is born, unto us a Son is given. 31

THE GIFT OF FAITH In 1955 I had my first summer assignment as a seminarian. And I also had to make my first sick call.

Since I had just arrived in this small town on the prairies of Alberta, I did not yet know the woman who was in the hospital. Actually, it was not a hospital, but a medical clinic with a few beds. The woman had had a miscarriage.

It did not go as well as I had hoped. First, she was much younger than I had expected. I don't know why I had thought she would be as old as my mother. But she was young. Further, she talked English while I had expected her to speak Dutch. So I had my wrong Bible translation with me. There were also immediate complications: she seemed to be resigned to the loss of her baby, but her husband and she had had one cow, and that animal had died in the same week. The fear of poverty was in her voice.

I remembered an older minister telling me: "It's not hard to visit the sick. Sickness makes the saints of God mellow. But be sure to keep an eye on the poor. Poverty makes people bitter."

My first patient was both ill and poor. And I did not have a handle on either temptation.

Then she said to me: "I've just been thinking that God must love John and me a lot. Because the Lord says he loves those he chastises."

That line had been going through my mind already. But I thought it would be too trite to use it. I was not going to be one of those preachers who dispense cheap comfort at bedsides.

Then she looked at me. And I saw that she was not cynical or bitter. She really meant it! Her face was a mixture of smile and sadness, and wisdom, that I have seen a thousand times since. It is the soft glow in troubled waters. She was leaning on God. She really believed that God chastened her because he loved her and John.

In that moment I became more of a Calvinist than I had been all year in seminary. I saw it with my own eyes: faith is a gift.

It was a humble seminarian who walked away from his first sick call. I had come with empty hands, holding only the wrong Bible version. Now I was so full that I needed to be alone.

33

SPIRITUAL BUTTERFLIES

Whenever you and I are talking about the imperfections of the church and the spiritual immaturity of many church members, we must recall that we did not always have what we now possess. We must not forget our past.

Every butterfly used to be a creepy caterpillar. I wonder if butterflies remember their past. If so, they must be a humble and compassionate lot.

Many spiritual butterflies forget the minute they get out of their cocoons what creeps and crawlers they were. Suddenly everyone else is guilty for not yet having flown above the flowers.

I remember a young man who belonged to a church a bit to the right of ours, if you know what I mean. He took me and my church to task for keeping in good and regular standing members who paid their dues to "godless labor unions." Apart now from his argument, I kept thinking that ten years earlier this man had been a member of a church I pastored. At that time I had to admonish him because he had been too rowdy and a little drunk at the annual fair in town. I did not remind him of his crawling existence, and I hoped that God was pleased with his butterfly.

Of course, we must never accept the status quo (the way things happen to be), certainly not in the church. We must constantly strive and push for spiritual maturity. But the way we go about the promotion of growth is as important to success as our goals themselves. We must even try to remember, but without guilt feelings, the sins God has forgiven.

I confess that I can be very irritated by spiritual immaturity within the church. But I must check my judgments carefully. Certainly, I must remember that young people and adolescents have a right to be immature. The best they can be is good, Christian, immature people. And God wants a sixteen-year-old to be a Christian sixteen-year-old.

It's more difficult to be patient with those from whom you might expect spiritual maturity because they are ripe in every other aspect. Here, too, we ought to remember that wisdom does not come with age, although I was told so when I was young. Aging is natural, getting wisdom isn't. You don't have to do anything to grow old. But growing up requires hard work, pain, prayer, and discipline.

No matter how spiritually mature we may be, two things are sure: we must be forever grateful that we were not kicked out of the company of the butterflies when we were still creepy crawlers; and, we still have a long way to go before God gives us a new set of wings.

MAILBOX Now that I am editor of *The Banner* I enjoy the fulfillment of ambitions I cherished for years: I have my own desk, my own office, and a real live secretary who tries to organize my life. But the important thing I always wanted was to get mail *every* day. Today that longing is fulfilled. I get mail on *every* working day and double on Mondays. And I love it.

When I count my blessings, after the mail carrier has left (nice job these people have!), I remember all of you who did not get any mail. I still know how a person can suffer when the mail passes you by.

When I had my mail drought, I used to invent ways of getting mail. I pass these on, though the reader must use these methods at personal risk. When *Readers Digest* offers a book for ten cents for the privilege of sending you another, do it. Send them a dime, get the book, but don't forget to return the other book as soon as it comes—or pay the bill. Now you are also on a mailing list and for the next ten years you will get letters flattering and cajoling you into buying and subscribing. Use your discretion.

If you subscribe to one national magazine, you will soon get letters from other magazines. I think they are all in cahoots. These letters will tell you that such an educated, discerning, smart person as yourself ought to subscribe to still another magazine. Of course, you don't have to do it. But it's nice to get a letter.

If you have a life insurance policy, even if it is for as small an amount as I used to have, you get a letter on every birthday. Life insurance people are more conscientious about remembering your birthday than your own children.

Of course, no mail, certainly no advertising, can ever take the place of real letters written by people you know. There is something movingly beautiful about someone sitting down, one hundred, two thousand, or thirty miles away, and writing a letter to you. And few scenes are more poignant than the little tragedies enacted by thousands of citizens all across the land evey day of the week: there she goes to the mailbox, winged by hope. She looks in it, she feels in it, she drops the lid on it, and returns dejectedly. "No mail."

Perhaps it also holds for letters that it is more blessed to send them than to get them. If that is so, my natural attitude toward the mailbox has often been sub-Christian.

I still feel bad that I did not write my mother more often. If you still have a mom, you should write her a letter tonight.

SEX AND COLD POTATOES

Divorce is never a solution to a bad marriage. It's merely the legal termination of a bad marriage.

Divorce may not be avoidable in all cases. It is a solution in no case. One cannot call the amputation of a bad leg the solution to an intolerable situation. But it is the end of that situation.

The church may not cease to love and nurture those who have failed in their marriage. First, because many divorced people are blameless. Second, if the church would proceed to remove all failures, no church would be left.

At the same time, we must intensify our war on the sins that destroy the beauty of our sexuality and of the institution of marriage. We must do that by cultivating the goodness of sexuality and marriage in the wholeness of a life that is redeemed by God.

Life that precedes marriage is as important to the success of marriage as the learning within marriage.

Once I shared a waiting room with two students of a Christian college. A young woman walked through the room, asked a question, and left again. The two young men looked at each other, grinned knowingly, and one said: "Feed my chickens." Both laughed—lecherously, I thought.

Let's assume that she did not know how sexily she walked and dressed and, further, that they did not know how worldly they looked and thought. For charity's sake, let's assume they aren't all three fully engaged in the Game.

I mean to say that those who play the funny-bunny-sexy games before marriage make poor spouses in the marriage. And those who learn to respect persons and love people make better husbands and better wives.

There was a boy in hot pursuit of a girl, the daughter of a friend of mine. The young man came for his fourth date in five days when her father caught him at the door of the car. "Before you go out," he said, "I'd like to ask you a question. What color are Betty's eyes?" "The color of Betty's eyes...well, of course they are bl—br—they are...."

"Young man," said the father, "there will be no date tonight."

I don't know if dad succeeded in keeping Betty from her suitor. But I don't blame him for stepping in to protect his daughter from a young man who had not yet lifted his eyes high enough to see the girl's eyes, let alone to see still higher matters.

One must feel sorry for our youth nowadays who get so much thrown at them, and so soon. It makes a lot of older people keel over. I do pray that we can show them, within the church, a picture of marital bliss that makes all the sizzling sex scenes of Satan seem like ten cents worth of cold potatoes.

VOWS AND FEELINGS

We must learn to accept divorced people as warmly as we have always embraced the bereaved. But while we embrace the bereaved, we know that we, too, are going to die. While we accept the divorced, we swear that we will never get a divorce.

Last night my wife and I were talking about three ministers and their wives, all friends of ours. Each of these couples have a child who is either separated or divorced. We thought about their parental pride and pain. And we prayed for our friends. We don't know the children as well as we know the parents. We are sure, however, that the children received Christian teaching about marriage as well as a Christian model of marriage. And yet the marriages went wrong.

One of my friends said that he no longer believes that all marriages are made to last. Some were based on error, he said, and to continue the marriage is to multiply misery. I am not ready to take that position. Of course, I've been involved, pastorally, in some marriages where one despairs of a solution. But I refuse to see divorce as a "solution."

In San Diego divorces are granted to a roomful of people at one and the same time. I saw it on TV last summer. The people, all suing for divorce, swear an oath(!) that they have irreconcilable differences, and they repeat, almost as in a church service, that this is the whole truth. Then the legal dissolution is pronounced.

This procedure may be better than long-lasting, exasperating, and costly divorce proceedings. But the sight of a roomful of people, ending with a solemn oath what they began with equally solemn vows, is full of pain and absurdity.

I don't think that there is any married person who did not think of quitting at one time or another. All of us have had some fleeting moments, or hours, maybe even weeks, when, at the edges of our consciousness, we sensed that it would be a vast relief to break up and to break out. People have these thoughts with respect to their marriages and some have them with respect to their very lives.

At such moments you must have something in your life that is stronger than your feelings and deeper than your hurts. It is the sacredness of the vow and the holiness of an action in which God was involved.

A million couples, who have grown old together, had the same problems young couples have. But they knew that vows are more durable than feelings.

One elderly couple wrote to us last Christmas, "We are now in the most beautiful times of our lives."

TO CATCH A THIEF

Supermarket cashier Linda Hollins was going to deposit a bag with more than one thousand dollars in Commerce Union Bank, somewhere in the state of Tennessee. A thief grabbed the bag and started to run toward his getaway car. But some people saw the act of robbery, and they turned the parking lot of the bank into a derby, trying to knock down the thief. Noted among the four or five cars that were chasing the robber was one black car, driven by a "fiercely determined elderly woman" that nearly took the life of the hapless thief. Finally the police got in and arrested their man.

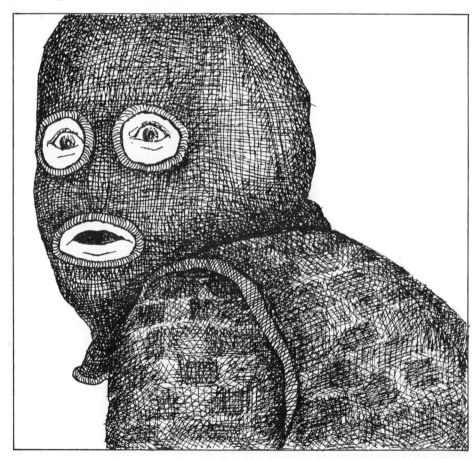

Such stories give me a deep sense of satisfaction.

I also remember an attempted holdup of a bank in Hamilton, Ontario. A man pulled a gun and said: "This is a stickup, hand over the money." But a truck driver who had been standing in line, gave the would-be thief a karate chop, and everyone except the thief was out of danger. Later the truck driver admitted that he had no training in karate or boxing, but that he had acted in anger. Although I read this story in the paper, I used to tell it at the dinner table as if I myself were present in the bank building.

As I said, such stories make me feel good. And I cringe when I read accounts of people being attacked, beaten, and robbed within earshot of normal citizens who don't bother to come to the rescue.

Vandalism, theft, murder, and all sorts of criminal acts are accepted as ordinary occurrences in most parts of North America. Far too few people are willing to join ranks with the "fiercely determined elderly woman" and give chase simply because something is horribly wrong and one cannot allow it to happen.

Our deepest wish is not that a thief gets caught, but that he or she gets converted. There must have been former robbers in the Ephesians church: "Let the thief no longer steal but rather, let him labor, doing honest work with his hands, so that he may be able to give to those in need" (4:28). That's ideal: from thieves to deacons. That's the converted lifestyle, and it does not seem that today's thieves learn the new style in today's prisons. We should all help Chuck Colson and show that we not only hate theft, but also love thieves for the sake of Jesus who died between two of them.

Meanwhile, if the theft of goods is merely another item to be calculated into the price ordinary consumers pay in the supermarket, we are bowing to the inevitable. Fear for a nation that cannot get angry anymore.

I know that anger is not the most fruitful response to a bad situation. But we will never find a solution to the present evil if we are not even capable of showing indignation.

FLORIDA   At 6:30 A.M. it is very quiet on the beaches of southern Florida. The sun is not yet above the horizon, but the white and orange sky is announcing its coming.

An old Toyota pulls up in the parking lot at the edge of the beach. An elderly woman gets out of the car. She puts on heavy gloves, takes some plastic garbage bags from the backseat, and goes to a refuse container that is sitting against a retaining wall. She begins to sort through the stuff in the container, picking out aluminum cans. And great is her harvest.

The garbage is not smelly, really, because although Finders Lounge fills a container every day, it is emptied the next morning before nine o'clock by a big collector's truck that lifts the whole thing and dumps the contents in its belly.

I help the woman by collecting some cans around the lounge. These cans had been tossed in the sand or against the building. Quite a few are standing upright and many of them are almost full of beer. I ask the woman if she finds many cans that are more than half-full. Yes, she does. "I guess they are so far gone, they don't know anymore what they are paying for."

This state has no deposit on cans and bottles; therefore, the public parks are littered to the point where many areas can no longer be enjoyed. The woman gathers aluminum cans and takes them to a recycling station. She used to wash the cans by hand, but now she throws them in the yard and washes them with a garden hose. Then she lets them lie in the sun for a day. It does not pay much, "but it pays for the gas." Her children don't like it that she goes out collecting cans. "But sitting at home, doing nothing, drives me nuts." I say that more people should be touched by her spirit. "It's the way my mother raised me."

Now a fisherman comes onto the beach. His fishing poles are taped to his bike. Nearly everyone who fishes in Florida uses at least two lines.

The sun is coming up. But the fisherman is fussing with his reel. And the woman does not take her eyes off the beer cans.

44

I watch the takeoff of the mighty ball. For half an hour the sky heralds its launching. But once it begins to lift from the ocean, the whole disc is free from the water in less than a minute. Then you cannot look at it much longer. The sun's rays sweep over the beach and knock on the windows of the luxury apartments. Behind those windows countless people over sixty are now beginning to wonder what they are going to do with another day.

Another day of grace. God's sun shines on the evil and on the good and on a million beer cans along the beaches of Florida.

MOTHER'S DAY The three mothers I know best are my own mother, my wife, and my daughter.

My mother *lived* motherhood. That was her one and only vocation. When we, her children, now talk about it, we are inclined to say that "she had no life of her own."

She lived and believed in days when family planning was considered to be sin. She had twelve children. She was pregnant for one hundred and eight months of the sixty-four years she lived on this earth. Her first child died at birth. The others were all healthy. One was killed in an accident.

My mother was the most self-effacing person I have ever known. 46 She loved the Lord, her husband, and her children, and she had no time for herself. Each of her children got organ lessons for three winter seasons; everyone had to know a song for every Monday in the Christian school; everyone had to learn a text for Sunday school. She always insisted that we bring home many friends on Saturdays and Sundays, and that we help Dad every other day of the week as soon as we came out of school. She had no vacations and bought nothing for herself until my sister was old enough to make her do so.

She literally spent herself on her children. She knew no greater joy than to see us well-behaved and happy. I am sure that her deep piety was the source of her life. But she was also shaped by a particular cultural understanding of God's will: motherhood was her vocation.

She died while she was about to set the table. She just fell down and was no more. And she looked like a queen, said my father.

My wife amazed me when she became a mother. Until that time she was certainly not the motherly type, I thought. But she took to motherhood so naturally, and, it seemed to me, so wisely, that I felt a new kind of feeling for her.

We have half the number of children my parents had.

My wife is a terrific mother. Our children will bear witness.

However, she is quite different from my mother, simply because she is not my mother and because she lives in a different time. She has been bombarded by all the ideas that make mothers and homemakers feel like the fraying fringes of humanity. My wife is too smart to believe that stuff, but something always rubs off. Anyway she not only insisted that our lives should not be entirely wrapped up in our children, but she also made room in her personal life to be more than a mother.

And then my daughter, who is now expecting her third. When I can take my eyes off my grandchildren long enough to look at her, I marvel that such a sophisticated person could suddenly learn skills that are age-old and that appear to be brand-new.

Women change with the times. Every age gives them a new chance and a new style of being female. But motherhood is ageless. Mothers get their wisdom directly from God.

LOST SHEEP   The greatest sadness among our readers is not caused by death, the natural death all of us must die. The greatest pain is suffered when loved ones seem to be heading for eternal death.

I know a large number of people who have a son or daughter, sister or brother, who does not love the Lord. These people will say: "She does not go to church." But you and I know what is meant! "She has broken the covenant, denied the Savior, and, as far as we know, has no future."

From our Bible reading we know that this situation is to be expected. The Lord has said that family unity would be torn apart by the division he brought into the world.

People are saying that this situation is much more prevalent than it used to be. I don't know if that is true. Perhaps people had no choice in the close-knit community of a previous generation. Maybe it was impossible to get off the tribal train. Today we are mobile, scattered, exposed to all sorts of influences.

Parents can feel terribly guilty when one of their children breaks the covenant. There's always the nagging question: "What did we do wrong?"

Although no sensitive parents would claim that they did a perfect job, there's often no reason to be haunted by guilt when one of the children refuses the claims of the Savior. We may rest in the forgiveness of our shortcomings, and we must realize that our grownup children have their personal responsibility.

Parents remain defensive of their children because they love them. Therefore they will explain the wrong behavior of their John or Jane. They will say harsh words about the church; they will say that the other sons and daughters of the congregation, who were in the youth clubs with their John and Jane, were less honest than John and used to pick on Jane. It will seem to the onlookers and other church members that these parents are approving their children's unfaithfulness and blaming everyone else. But you must remember that these parents are hurting inside and praying every night.

48

Parental love cannot give up. It hopes against hope and believes against reason. Parents cannot help loving children who have offended God. It is a powerless love that would do anything to help, if only it could. "Absalom, Absalom, would I had died instead of you, Absalom, my son!" Yet this love comes closest to the powerful and effective love of him who gave his life to save us from death. And since Christ is still here, and his love still active, there are no hopeless cases.

EVANGELICAL HANDBOOK ON EATING

There was a time when eating and drinking were the regular delights in the daily routine of ordinary people. This is no longer the case in North America. Nutritionists and moralists have intruded into our kitchens and dining rooms. They have turned us into fearful eaters.

I don't mind nutritionists as long as they remain technical. Then they can be as useful as dentists and auto mechanics. But most of our dieticians become moralists. They put the fear of Hades into ordinary diners.

There is a growing list of "how to eat" books by evangelical authors. Pious people buy them. And once these books lie on the refrigerators in the kitchens of the faithful, they moralize and tyrannize the whole kitchen.

You must be careful with these evangelical gurus. They pick one Bible text about food but they never explain why they skip another one.

Daniel refused the "king's dainties," as they are called in the older Bible versions. He made a wager with the king's official: let us have water and vegetables for ten days. If we don't look better than those who eat from the royal menu, after a ten-day test, you may do with us as you see fit.

Most manufacturers of miracle diets would not dare stick out their necks that far.

Daniel and his friends did well with their kosher foods. After ten days they looked better and knew more than all the magicians and enchanters.

But Paul said that all the foods are kosher, though not for everybody.

There was one man in the Old Testament who had his diet prescribed and delivered by heaven. When Elijah was hiding at the brook, God sent him two meals a day, bread and meat, by means of the ravens. Does this mean that breakfast and supper is enough and we should cut out lunch?

Now, if you can say what the story of Daniel teaches us about the kind of foods we should eat, and the story of Elijah about the number of meals we should have, you are well on your way to writing an evangelical handbook on eating.

Watch out for moralists. They used to stand on pulpits. Now they write cookbooks and government literature. They tell you how you should look and feel, what and how you should eat, and how to—yes, how to live!

I plead for liberated kitchens where ordinary people have their regular delights in the daily routine. "Lord, bless this food to our use, and use us to be a blessing."

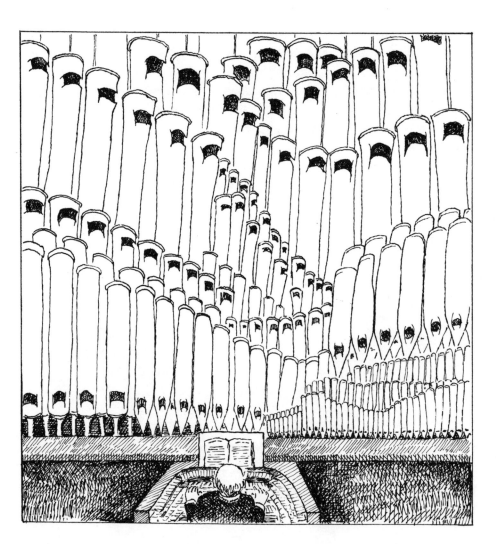

TOO MUCH ORGAN

An organ is an imitation of a wide range of musical instruments. When you pull out a stop, you add a piccolo or an oboe or a trumpet. And when you pull out all the stops, you have a whole orchestra.

For reasons I have never yet investigated, organs are as intimately connected with the life and worship of the church as pews and pulpits.

I love organs, but I don't love them as much now as I did years ago.

One reason for my diminishing love is some bad organists (who spoil it for the good ones); but the main reason is the sort of superstitious attachment congregations have developed toward this mechanical instrument. I believe it is high time that, at least once a month, we keep the organ locked and try to worship God without it.

Organ players are among the most devoted Christians and church people. I am sure that in our colleges, Calvin and Dordt, where we have huge organs in beautiful halls, students are taught that organ music must help and not hinder worship. Organists must educate but not dominate the singing of the congregation. No doubt the vast majority of them know this and attempt to practice it. In at least one congregation I served as pastor, we had an organist who contributed immeasurably to every worship service. And most others made contributions to many services.

The trouble is that some worshipers lean on the organ so heavily in their efforts to worship God that they feel bereft and distraught when the organ does not play. They feel awkward and naked when, during the singing, their words of praise and confession are not overshadowed by organ tones. And they feel ill at ease when, before the service and between the parts of the liturgy, their speech is not covered up by the "religious" tones of the organ.

People really believe that an organ (certainly a pipe organ) is a religious instrument. Among poorly educated congregations, objections will be raised to the accompaniment of a piano, an oboe, and certainly a guitar; but an organ is hallowed. And among financially poor congregations I have witnessed disproportionate investments in pipe organs.

Beauty without truth is a hoax. When the preacher covers up the Word of truth with human talk, the elders (first) and the congregation must demand to hear God's truth. And when the organ music becomes a blanket coverage for the congregation's religious expression, we should switch off the organ so that God can hear the truth.

SNOOPERVISION

A nearby community is in uproar because a porn shop is being established there against the wishes of most of the citizens.

I was struck by the faith of the operator of the shop. He is confident that he will be able to start his business because the law allows him to peddle his dirty wares (he has been in court often enough to know it), and he is confident that he will get plenty of business because most people love sinful thrills.

He is right on that last point. Most of us love forbidden fruit.

If we could put you in a room with only two magazines, *The Banner* and a magazine from the porn shop, and if you were absolutely sure no one was observing you, which one of the two magazines would you pick up?

Of course, God would see you in that room. Somehow, however, that does not seem to frighten most of us.

A Jewish rabbi was dying, and his disciples crowded around his bed, crying: "Oh, master, give us a last word, some last wisdom, father!" Then the dying rabbi said: "May you always live as if the neighbors were observing you."

The rabbi's students were very disappointed. This piece of wisdom was much more shallow than the heavenly gem they were begging for.

As a matter of fact, we are kept from countless ills because we keep an eye on each other. Many trusting parents have been astonished to learn how their children behave when they are not being observed by Mom or Dad. But also grownups need the looks of the neighbors, the mutual censure of the church community, and the company of spouse or friends to stay on the straight and narrow. We complain about this type of "snoopervision," and we long to get away from it now and then; but do we ever need it!

Yes, it is a sign of our immaturity when we still give in to that old inclination to sin when Mom and Dad are not around. But it is better to admit our weakness (many spouses would be alcoholics if their partners had not helped them) than to fall into a deep hole.

I admire people who travel on a single ticket and live upright Christian lives. Often they have more temptations and opportunities to sin than people who travel in pairs.

And here is some more rabbinical advice: may you learn to fear the eyes of God more than the glances of the neighbors.

THE CRACK IN THE CONCRETE

While we were driving from Grand Rapids to Holland, Michigan, my wife spotted a sunflower that was growing out of a crack in the concrete road about a foot from the freeway railing. It was an amazingly defiant yellow flower on a long stem.

The sight of the flower sent a message to that mysterious computer God has built: my memory bank. One punch retrieved a story that had not been on the screen of my mind for, oh, maybe forty-five years. I heard my third-grade teacher reading a story about a boy with a peashooter. One of his peas landed in the crack of a windowsill. Behind the window was a sick child who was always in bed. This child was then entertained by the plant that grew out of the crack in the windowsill.

All the stories my teacher read were intended to work together for good. This particular story taught us about the wonder of growth and the even greater wonder of God's love for a sick child whose dreary life was cheered by a plant that grew by the God-directed seed dropped into the crack of the windowsill.

First I was amazed by the sunflower in the concrete highway, then I marveled even more at the story that came back to me after so many years. Look how we are programmed: "Seed in crack grows plant" is the message from my eyes to my brain. The brain sifts through half a century of impressions and memories stored in its bank. Quickly it sends a film message to the screen of my mind. I see the teacher in third grade and hear the story about "seed in crack grows plant." All of that within one second.

While we continued to drive over that freeway, we talked about our local church's Vacation Bible School, which was to start the following week. The school meets for only five mornings, but it takes an enormous amount of planning and preparation. Then you wonder how much you can teach to such a variety of children, many of whom have not had any religious instruction.

I said that I was in favor of teaching them a few good Christian songs that would stay with them long after Bible School ended. Once they know "Trust and Obey," they have the Christian message in a nutshell, and they might still be humming it next Christmas.

And I am in favor of telling some vivid stories about God and Jesus. Forty-five years later they'll be driving over some freeway and they'll see, smell, or feel something, and suddenly God will replay on the screen of their minds the story they heard in Bible school. You never know.

All the thousands of kids who were exposed to our Vacation Bible Schools this summer are now scattered over the asphalt and concrete jungles of our lands. Many will never enroll in our church schools, although I hope the churches try hard to get them. Yet God is able to cause a crack in the concrete and grow flowers that bring a message of the power and the glory.

GOD AND THE SALMON

Seldom was I so moved by God's general revelation as four or five years ago this October when I saw the salmon go up Gold Stream on Vancouver Island. It's called spawning season. Hundreds of fish jump the little waterfalls as strength allows. They come in pairs; the male urges the female on because she has to lay her eggs close to the source of the stream. Once they have swum far enough, they make a sort of nest in the gravel of the clear, shallow waters. Then the female lays her eggs—and both she and the male die.

It is a touching sight: the laying of eggs is the last act, terminating and perpetuating life. And in their death, the parents also serve the future generation: the decomposing fish are food for the young who break out of the eggs.

This part of Gold Stream (so called because people used to pan gold in the stream) is a provincial park. Wardens keep an eye on the tourists. They may not interfere with the pilgrimage of the salmon.

If this provincial park would consider appointing a chaplain at Gold Stream, I might want to apply.

One can hardly desire a more legible page in God's book of creation. And there ought to be a chaplain who would cry at the tourists: "Look and read, people. Behold and become wise!"

The wardens would be a big help in spreading the message because they explain the laws of God: these fish, they say, have been away from their birthplace for an average of four years. They have been swimming through rivers and cruising the ocean. But now you see them return on their last voyage. They can hardly make it because they are rapidly deteriorating. Look, their color is not healthy and their strokes no longer vigorous. But they must go on. By higher law they are commanded to move to their final appointment. So, they obey without hesitation. Persistently they attempt the next jump and still another current. Unerringly they know their destiny.

If I were a preacher along Gold Stream, I would want to open the other Book too. If I could get the tourists' attention and the park's permission, I would climb a tree and read Jeremiah 8:7:

"Even the storm in the heavens knows her times; and the turtledove, swallow, and crane" [here I would insert: "and the salmon"] keep the time of their coming; but my people know not the ordinance of the Lord."

At Gold Stream people must wonder: what do the salmon know that we have forgotten?

61

FIGHT SIN AND IGNORANCE

Our battle is not only against sin but also against stupidity. Battling ignorance requires more time and energy from elders, pastors, and editors than fighting immorality. The peace and progress of many churches are disturbed more often by the absence of wisdom than by sinful deeds of its members.

Perhaps you find this hard to believe but in my first congregation we lost a member because the flowers from a wedding ceremony on Saturday had remained in church during the Sunday morning service. The offended party was opposed to "decorating God's house." Debate was long and pointless.

I know a couple who left the church because other people took their seats in a particular pew. People got angry; the angels were weeping.

One man in my second congregation refused to attend church unless I would read from the King James Version of the Bible. I was on the verge of giving in, but the consistory said no. The consistory was right. But I thought that the brother had at least some pious concern that should be honored. I wasted a number of calls on him. I pleaded with him and got angry at him. I challenged him to explain to me 2 Corinthians 6:12 from the King James Version. But he kept saying that this was the only translation made by godly men and approved by the Spirit. He left our church.

This side of glory we will be unable to eradicate sin and stupidity. But we should fight them both with God's weapons—incessantly.

How does one fight ignorance? By training in godliness, by broadening the perspective of Christians, and by sharpening their focus on Christ.

This Christian education must take place at the right time. The above-mentioned examples of stupidity show that some idea or custom became unalterably fixed in the victim's dimly lit scale of religious values. Education should have preceded confrontation. There is a point in the human development, or lack of it, where people, like old dogs, cease to be learners. They don't discuss anymore; they snarl.

Woe to the teachers who do not teach today!

Many members of our church, who are otherwise well educated, will accept no other norms for their Christian faith and actions than those they received from their grandparents. For them it is impossible to be biblically critical of whatever they learned at mother's knee. And I fear that some pastors and teachers like to keep their people that way.

The church chokes in ignorance unless every new generation has a firsthand knowledge of Jesus, fresh from the pages of the Book.

TEENAGERS   Let me try, just once more, to give you my collected wisdom on the topic of teenagers. Then I'll keep quiet about this subject. And that silence ought to show that I know what I am *not* talking about.

The big difference between teenagers and grownups is that grownups cannot look at things without seeing the consequences. That spoils a lot of fun, or prevents a lot of trouble, depending on your viewpoint.

We parents think of marriage and offspring as soon as our teen-

64

ager has his or her first date. After the second date, we might even broach the subject. The teenager finds our thinking "ridiculous," "silly," or, when a senior in high school, "preposterous." But we think of the consequences not only of dating but of everything.

When our teenage daughter begins to enjoy the glances of the opposite sex, she will dress in a way that enrages her father. He gets enraged because he knows so much more than his daughter does. She will accuse him of having a "filthy mind." The confrontation may end with a tearful, budding woman in a different set of clothes. And when the dark of night has made all things quiet, Dad will realize that his daughter behaved without malice.

Individually, teenagers are some of the nicest creatures God ever made. Collectively, they are a threatening mass of humanity, ruled by glands and by social and chemical reactions. Come to think of it, one could also say that of other groups.

The idea that teenagers should have separate instruction, even in church, and a separate social life, even in the basement at home, is a bad one. It is even worse than the idea that senior citizens should be removed to an isolated corner—because teenagers need the older ones worse than the other way around. Besides, teenage parties are louder than senior-citizen ones.

Teenagers are always fighting forces they don't quite understand and enjoying fun without thinking of the consequences. But they also surrender themselves to sorrow as if it has no limits. They don't quite know that there is an end to pleasure, but they also fail to understand that pain lasts but a season.

When I observe them, I can feel very concerned and compassionate—a typical adult reaction. But when I read books about them, I almost despair, and I wonder how my wife and my brothers and sisters and I ever made it through that period without irreparable harm. We made it because Dad and Mom were always somewhere in the background of that happiest times of our lives.

And God was there.

NO RETAKES   Films can be so unnaturally perfect because directors shoot the same scene as often as seven times or more. Then the film editors splice the actors' best performance into the film. The viewers never see the boo-

boos and mistakes. The audience never hears the wrong words and the bad expressions. Those scenes have been cut.

Life does not offer these opportunities. All of us play our roles but once. No retakes. When the year has rolled by, many of us might want to say to the camera operator: "Let me redo August 27" or "Let me have another try at the afternoon of December 25." But what is past is past; it is not gone, really, but it is unalterable.

Our blunders can be forgiven, but they cannot be removed. They are engraved on the films of our lives and printed in the recorders of heaven. My film has many blunders and quite a few transgressions. And I have asked God to strike many a line from the record. The word *Forgiven* is stamped large on the calendar of my days. But I can never go back to former days and try again.

We are locked into the framework of time. We move inexorably forward. There is no "reverse," and we cannot step out. We can think it over, of course, but we cannot *do* it over. Every moment that is past is frozen solid. But every day that is ahead must still be given shape.

Since all of us are such blunderers, we have moments when we resent that this process of time cannot be repeated. When I was very small, I used to play checkers with my grandfather, and whenever he lost he would say: "We'll play another game." But the game of life cannot be played a second time.

The notion that all of us will have a "second chance" must have been born out of resentment. Others will say that it arose from a sense of fair play: because we have an unequal number of marbles when we start.

There won't be a chance to "do it over." Our Maker has made it quite clear that this one life is conclusive, as "the life in the flesh." But one might say that this life is but a rehearsal for the great performance that is coming.

Moving through time (that is, living) is such serious business not only because we cannot move back, but because we will reap tomorrow what we sow today.

IT'S EASIER THE SECOND TIME

Newspapers report that two actresses, Elizabeth Taylor and Zsa Zsa Gabor, have each been married and divorced seven times. That's even worse than the woman Jesus met at the well; she had been married five times and was living wtih number six.

In case we meet Taylor or Gabor at the water cooler, you and I must remember to be as friendly as Jesus was. Both of these women badly need the living water; it's the only way to quench their insatiable thirst.

The second time goes easier; this holds for both good and evil acts. I had a friend who seemed to be the happiest husband and father you can imagine; his marriage lasted about fifteen years. But once he had broken with his wife and the church, he married and divorced in quick succession.

This week I was reading a report of the diaconal organization in the Kalamazoo area. These people do much good work that depends on volunteers. The deacons say that once a person has volunteered for a certain job, this person usually comes back to do it again. If you have never done a diaconal job (fixed a porch for someone, delivered goods to a family, took some kids to dinner, drove someone to the doctor's office), it seems like an impossible hassle. Once you have done it, you say: I want to do that again.

Thus good and bad barriers in our lives keep us from doing what we have never done before.

If you have never stolen and never been unfaithful to your spouse, keep it that way. Never get proud of your good behavior and pray that God keeps the door locked. Don't even allow yourself to play with the thought of stealing money or cheating on your spouse. It takes less pain and power to stay within the borders than to be restored to the good path once you have crossed God's boundaries.

But there are also people who have never expanded themselves in doing good works. They have never talked to anyone about Jesus, they have only entertained their buddies, and they have never given a really worthwhile gift to God. They live within tradition-made barriers, and they don't know how meaningful life could be if they would knock down the partitions.

Try it. The second time goes easier.

69

MUSIC IN CHINA

Ninety percent of the movies now being shown are probably not worth seeing, and I have viewed very few of the other 10 percent. But I did go to see *From Mao to Mozart*, a film about the trip of violinist Isaac Stern to Red China.

This film is entertaining and enriching. Moreover, it gives some hope to a world that is constantly suffering from international tensions. The Chinese loved Isaac Stern. They filled every chair in every auditorium where he performed. And common love for beautiful music created a joy that was tangible in the little theater in which I saw the film: when the Chinese clapped, an elderly woman behind me also started to applaud.

Stern is a virtuoso on the fiddle and a masterful teacher. Talented young players tried out in his hearing. Stern corrected and encouraged them. His enthusiasm and humor, his quick violin lessons and short talks, were a genuine delight.

The viewer cannot forget the conservatory professor who was locked up in a closet for fourteen months during the cultural revolution in China. His crime was that he taught Western, that is, classical European, music. A number of his colleagues committed suicide during that wave of barbarism because they could not bear the humiliation inflicted on them.

Now, however, says the film, China has turned from Mao to Mozart. It is indeed a song of hope, orchestrated by Isaac Stern and his accompanist.

Classrooms full of zealous and disciplined Chinese are shown not only making music but also engaging in dance, gymnastics, and ping pong. I loved them and admired the potential for good.

I know that the Chinese and the Americans need more than music to inherit the kingdom. But music makes for international joy and understanding. And we are delivered from bestiality when our ears and eyes are open to beauty.

The world will climax with a concert before the throne of God. And when the harps and violins are handed out, I hope to sit close to some of those Chinese people I saw in the film.

STATISTICAL EVIDENCE

Most "statistical evidence" is not based on actual counting but on educated guesses and scientific samples.

It is a riddle to me how anybody can know in the morning what percentage of the population watched a televised program on the previous evening. Yet those who rate a TV program are never proved wrong and their "ratings" are the gods of the industry. They are never shown up as liars because they give figures concerning yesterday's happenings. Political pollsters predict the future. Their work is hazardous. They have made some terrible mistakes. But America never paused long enough to laugh the pollsters out of the land.

Today statistics are available on every conceivable topic. The media tell us how many doctors recommend what pill, what percentage of people sleep on their right side, how many snore, how many squeeze and roll the toothpaste tube and how many merely squeeze; and how many of us are born again.

In 1962 a study in New York City reported that Jews are fatter than Roman Catholics, that Catholics are more obese than Protestants and that, among the Protestants, the Baptists are the heaviest and the Episcopalians, the thinnest.

I have no faith in statistics. One reason for my disbelief is that I have never been asked a single question in any one of the ten thousand polls being reported. Neither has my wife ever been asked whether she could part with her favorite detergent or how she likes the President. My children have never been asked about TV programs, about sexuality or fidelity, and yet every one of us is always included in the "statistical evidence."

My suspicion is that these statistics are not so much information about habits and opinions, but tools to form habits and opinions. Especially when the polls concern behavior and belief, conduct and attitudes, the results are used to nudge us into a certain direction—usually the wrong direction.

If Ahab and Jezebel would have had pollsters and court statisticians (and maybe they did), the ratings for Baal would have been 100 percent minus one old pesky prophet of the Lord. Elijah himself believed the polls. He asked the Lord to take him off the list. Then God said: "My statistics show that there are seven thousand who did not bow their knees to Baal."

I trust the Lord to keep the record straight.

PRAYING TOGETHER

One out of three marriages in the Soviet Union ends in divorce, and a third of all divorces take place before the couple is married for one full year.

Even if we are suspicious of statistical information, we might be inclined to believe this statistic because it comes from Russia.

This week I heard of two more couples who are breaking up. Both couples are young. Reminders of the Soviet Union?

I admit that my wife and I had our worst squabbles in our first year. Maybe those spats weren't as bad as they seemed. But you know how a small tree behaves in a gust of wind. Twenty-nine years later it's easy to say that it was only a breeze.

How do you stay together?

If a couple would ask me I would answer without a moment's hesitation that they should pray together.

That answer would not make them happy. It's not the kind of advice people pay for. If I would say: "Wash together seven times in the Hubba Tubba," they would think I was giving them a secret love recipe. But when I say, "Pray together," they think they are getting the usual preacher's line.

I myself had to learn how to pray. When my wife and I had our first breakfast together, I said, "Let's pray silently." But she said: "No, we are married now; you should pray out loud." So, I said a prayer. I was embarrassed. And we had our first married people's breakfast. She expected me to pray, and I felt I could not get away from it because that's how we understood our roles. I was not a preacher, then, and I was not even planning to become one.

Now I say to John and Jane, "You must pray together." You must speak to God in an audible voice. Say: "*God, help Jane and me to love each other, for Jesus' sake, Amen.*" Then you open your eyes and you look at each other with love and fear; because those two emotions are never far apart. (At least, not until love is perfect, 1 John 4:18. But that takes more than twenty-nine years.)

74

I know very well that marriage is more than a prayer meeting. But people still marry because they love each other, if I understand rightly. And if you really have it, if you have *love*, you have got the sweetest thing God left in this fallen world. It's the last flower of paradise. It is different from anything else; and you know it.

Therefore, whatever else we may have to do in order to enrich our marriage (perk it up, put zing into it, or whatever), the best and basic thing is still to pray to God. He must protect his own gift. This flower is never safe in our hands.

HOLY FORGETFULNESS

Driving on a highway recently, I saw a sign: "Left Lane Closed 2,000 feet." That's a fair warning and one gets three or four more warnings before the lane is actually closed.

As it turned out, however, it was not the left lane but the right lane that was closed. I'm sure that sign was changed soon. And the road crew must have had a great time kidding those who did not know the difference between right and left.

Some of our children also had trouble knowing which hand was the right hand. One of them would always make a motion as if she were writing whenever she had to know which hand was her left and which was her right.

There are cases, according to the Bible, in which our hands, which always and automatically cooperate in pushing, lifting, and typing, should not know the acts of each other. "Do not let your left hand know what your right hand is doing" (Matt. 6:3).

Years ago there was a congregation in Canada where people used to say of their organist that his left hand never knew what his right hand was doing. And that was not intended to be a compliment.

But Christ was teaching how to give money when he gave that saying about the left and the right hand. In at least one consistory this text was the occasion for a long debate on the legitimacy of recording donations for income tax deductions. Those who thought that income tax deductions help the people of God to give more won the debate.

The point of Matthew 6:3 is that we should not calculate the credits we are gaining with God when we give of our money. We should exercise ourselves in holy forgetfulness when it comes to our good works. Then God won't forget.

I know that many people are forgetful when they spend money. Lots of people say at the end of the week: "I don't now where the money went." Those people never have any money to give.

Some of us go into restaurants and spend twenty dollars without giving it a second thought. But when one of us big spenders, in a moment of emotion, puts twenty dollars in the plate in church, chances are that he or she feels righteous for twenty days. And that's what the Lord was talking about.

Perhaps it is even more difficult to forget our own good works than it is to overlook the sins of others.

EASTER COMES IN SPRING

A veteran missionary to Nigeria, now retired and living in Michigan, does not feel that he made all the sacrifices people talk about. He enjoyed his work. But he did miss one thing for so many years: the changing of the seasons.

That's something we in the Dakotas, in Alberta, Iowa, and Ontario do not think about. None of us, all through last winter, said: those poor missionaries in Nigeria, the Philippines and Mexico, on whom the sun is shining every day. . . . Now, however, the miracle of spring is here. All who live in tropical countries are missing out on one of the greatest treats God prepared for us: creation is born again. Poor missionaries. May God make up to you by showing you the new birth of people. That's greater yet.

I cannot forget the many sermons I heard when I was young, warning that the event of the resurrection, commemorated at Easter, may not be traded for rabbits or the cycle of nature. And I trust that you and I would never want to do that.

At the same time, it is entirely fitting that we observe the feast of the new life in spring and that we celebrate Pentecost when the air is fragrant with new flowers. After all, according to Psalm 96, the church is a sort of choir director for the whole creation: "Say among the nations, 'The Lord reigns!' " Then the sea, the fields, and the trees must exult and sing for joy.

Don't you feel at least a little urge in your mouth and your muscles to begin the great cosmic song festival? I do.

I live a little more than a mile from my office. My wife and the doctor and my conscience say that I should walk. For months, however, I had the excuse of deep snow, a heavy briefcase, wetness, and/or ice. Now I am walking again. I cross a cemetery where hundreds of people are buried. Sometimes this makes me somber. But when the promise of spring is in the air, and when, so it seems to me, it may burst anytime, I say in a loud preacher's voice: "Soon the trumpet will sound." I walk ten steps, and I say: "Life is stronger than death." I look at a tombstone and proclaim: "Jesus has risen already."

Of course, I am all alone on my pathway through the cemetery. Actually, I am happy nobody hears me. If people heard me they might not believe Psalm 96 was being fulfilled. They might say: "Look at that fellow; spring has gone to his head."

WE NEED GRANDPARENTS

Our third daughter got married last Saturday. My wife and I have now acquired three sons through the efforts of our daughters. Every time we have accepted their choices with fear and trembling, but thus far we have learned to admire our daughters' tastes.

This bride looked very much like another woman at another wedding thirty years ago. That's not my prejudice; everybody said she looked like my wife.

This was also the first time in five years that all our children and grandchildren were together in one place. Normally they are scattered over three continents and four countries. So, the cup was full and running over.

What was particularly enjoyable—and that's what I wanted to write about—was the presence of grandparents, besides uncles, aunts, and other relatives.

Four of the eight grandparents of the bridal couple are still living, and they were at the wedding. One grandfather and one grandmother said a few words. Everybody listened attentively because together they have lived more than 150 years.

The grandfather closed his speech with a little Dutch poem that the just-married couple did not even understand. But they caught the sentiment as they were listening almost reverently. I, too, was listening and began to translate in my mind:

"Commit in trust your paths and all that gives you pains
to Him whose favor lasts who over all things reigns. . ."

I saw Grandmother embrace one of her grandsons whom she had not seen for a long time. He is a big man, and he had to crouch next to Grandma's chair. She put both arms around his neck, wept against his cheek, and whispered things about love and prayer.

It's good for us, in this rough and tumble world, to feel the arms of Grandma now and then. And we need the prayers of grandparents all the time.

Blessed is the church and blessed the clan whose grandparents keep a vigil of prayer.

Our need is not only for roots and the reassurance of the familiar. We need the eyes and hands of people who are now close to the top of Mount Nebo and to the vision of the Promised Land. They have traveled so long. They know what must be carried on the journey and what might as well be discarded.

81

MORE OF THE SAME Some time ago we had a reunion of the seminary class of '57. That's the class in which I graduated twenty-five years ago.

Not everyone could come, of course. Three have already joined the church triumphant. Some day all of us, I hope, will go to them and have the big reunion.

Twenty-two men and most of their wives came. All of us had been together for three years in seminary. Many of us had not seen much of each other since that time.

Everyone was allowed to make a "little" speech. Since all of us were ministers, this speechmaking may not have been such a good idea. My wife says it wasn't. As a result of twenty-two "little" speeches, we got home late, and we must always be up early.

The stories were very interesting, although some dwelt too long on the accomplishments of their children.

Did my classmates change much since their seminary days? They looked older, of course. A few seemed to be rather well preserved, but most of them looked as wrinkled and battered as I do.

However, on a deeper level, they had not changed much. It struck me that all of them are what they used to be in the seminary—only more so. The bashful one is still shy. The exuberant one is still in high spirits. The one who hated school is still throwing stones at eggheads. The serious one is more serious, and the studious one has made a career of it. The eloquent one has honed his skill. The one who was slow of speech twenty-five years ago is still searching for words. And when we sang the doxology at the close of the evening, standing in a circle and holding hands, I saw tears on the cheeks of the man who was emotional when we were in seminary.

Some people still get married with the hope of changing everything they don't like in their partners. "It will be different once we are married." I am the first one to admit that, if anything can change us, it is a love relationship with another person. But let's not imagine that we can re-make each other.

The greatest change comes over a person when he or she has a love relationship with Jesus Christ. A million people can tell you the difference that relationship makes in a person's behavior, ambitions, life! But even the Spirit of God does not erase the way God made us in the first place.

That's why seminarians, after twenty-five years, are still what they used to be; only more so.

HEAVEN OR HELL   Recently a man told me that I should write more about heaven and hell.

I was a bit evasive: "I know so little about those places." But he insisted: "Every one of your readers is going to spend eternity in heaven or in hell. You should scare them out of hell and show them the way to heaven."

"But I write about Jesus very often. He is the Way."

"Yeah, but you should write more directly, and you should hit harder."

I have done some thinking about his remarks. At first my inclination was to give the man a label and to file him away. Call him an other-worldly evangelical who thinks of salvation in terms of eternal life assurance.

Then I thought, our church paper is for Christian people. We assume that all of us believe in Christ and have eternal life.

But I did feel uneasy. Could it be true that we too often assume too much? Is it possible that ministers preach sermons but fail to raise the tough questions? Is it wholly imaginary that at family visiting elders discuss the church budget with an unsaved couple? Could a person read *The Banner* for forty years without ever being confronted with the question: "Dear reader, are you saved?"

Of course, some fellow Christians have irritated us because they are always asking the biggest question in the most casual conversations. We do not ask the question glibly, and we do not answer easily. Besides, we figure that, once our relationship to God has been settled by his grace, redeemed living is more important than safe dying.

But I have been impressed, lately, by the shortness of the present life.

I have also noticed that, except at funerals, we don't speak much of the future. Very few busy people tell me that the suffering of the present world is not worth comparing with the glory that will be revealed to them.

84   Some may have read so many books and met so many people that

the faith of the old evangelists has imperceptibly slipped away from them. Deep in their heart they don't believe anymore that there are only two ways and two exits.

Perhaps, then, we should ask each other the questions: Are you saved? Do you know where you are going?

This life is short. A person who has no future has nothing.

DEVIL IN CHURCH The Frisians have a saying to the effect that, if the sermon lasts longer than an hour, the devil comes into the church. The Rev. William Buursma, pastor of Third CRC in Kalamazoo, Michigan, has the saying hanging over the door through which he goes to mount the pulpit.

It's a wise saying. Maybe it is not as obviously scriptural as some of the other sayings and warnings that adorn lecterns and consistory rooms. "Sir, we wish to see Jesus" (John 12:21) is a more direct and literal admonition for the preacher to get to the point.

I don't know whether the Frisian text bears the translation: "If the *service* lasts more than an hour, the devil comes into the church." Probaby not. It says "sermon." Well, it must be a very old saying. The revised version should read that the devil comes into the church if the service lasts more than an hour.

Actually, I don't know if the devil gets in after the hour or if he manages to sneak in even earlier. I do know that the people want to get *out* when the hour is over. And it is probably true that the longer you keep the people in, the harder it is to keep the devil out.

The phrase, "devil in the church" in our Frisian text, means that the thoughts of the people are no longer captive by the Word. Some people are merely enduring the preacher. Others hate him. Most are bodily in the pew but they have mentally escaped. That's what the Frisians mean when they say, "the devil is in the church."

Well, brothers of the cloth, let's resist the devil and keep the sermons short. You older fathers and brothers, cut out your fifth illustration derived from an experience in your fourth congregation. You younger preachers, stop your babbling between the different parts of the liturgy; stick to the business of worship. And, for all of us, let not the multitude of our words dilute the potency of the Word. As to my fellow preacher who can find textual support for the worst of his habits, if you think that you must imitate Paul who once preached Eutychus to sleep, note then, at least, that this was Paul's farewell sermon to the congregation of Troas.

Suddenly I realize that some people are going to cut out today's column and mail it to their preachers. I cannot forbid it. But I may ask that you put your name on the envelope. Any pastor who gets this column from an anonymous sender may say: the devil got into my mailbox.

87

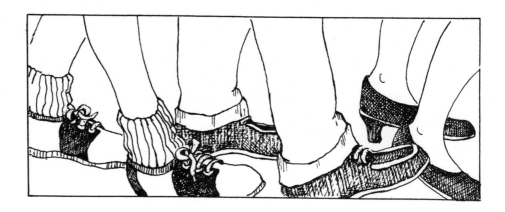

OUT OF STEP

Sometimes I have the feeling that I am out of step with society. I feel that I am a loner. There are moments when I think that everybody is intoxicated and I am sane, but it also happens that I fear that I am the only one who is abnormal. I wonder if other readers have that experience.

Perhaps it is due to my upbringing. For instance, my dad always said that you are rich when you pay your debts. So, I pay my invoices almost as soon as I get them and always before the due date. But I must be the only one who lives that way. Everyone else seems to be piling up invoices and then getting loans to pay them.

National economy is totally beyond my grasp, and it makes me sick when I am forced to think about it. I remember when I decided that I could not vote for Pierre E. Trudeau after he had been in office for about ten years. The debts of the country had increased so astronomically that I was sure we were heading for the poorhouse under his leadership.

Now I live in the United States, and the president is telling the people that the national debt is approaching a trillion dollars. That is one million times a million. It is such an incomprehensible amount that it fills me with apprehension. But the president looked very confident when he said he was going to do something about it. I was ready to help him. I was going to suggest that, if there are 250 million people in the country, and each would pay four thousand dollars, we could "pay our debts and be rich." Then he said we should all pay less taxes, and I

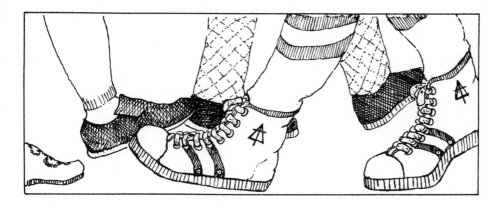

was totally baffled. At the time of this writing nothing has happened yet. The president's wife has put all new wallpaper in the White House. That's fine with me. I don't begrudge anybody any wallpaper. I did worry about the invoice, since we are so deep in the hole already.

No, I cannot live this way.

But that's not the only thing I have in mind when I say that I often feel that I don't fit in society. I have this feeling often right after I have seen the news on TV. The news is mostly tragic or infuriating. But the other day the announcer was happy as he told about a big feast: the president's oldest daughter by his first marriage got married for the third time in a very big wedding feast. Then there were reels of happy, even exuberant, people. Morosely I was looking at the screen, thinking of the pain of all the broken marriages—uneasy because everyone acted as if this were normal.

Even that one time, very recently, when we had the successful launching and landing of the spaceship Columbia and everybody was cheering, I was still out of step. Sure, I was happy; but I was still thinking, Why must they do that on a Sunday morning when all the computer operators, hundreds of thousands of spectators, and Young and Cripps themselves should have been in church?

Then I said to myself: the reason you are an unhappy loner is not that you are crazy or abnormal; you are Christian Reformed.

FEARFUL OR FIRM?   Teenagers are the most talked-about species of the last few decades. Market analysts, psychologists, and educators do most of the talking. But the parents of teenagers usually keep quiet.

I share the modesty of the parents. Looking back over one thousand sermons, I note that I was most outspoken on "How to Raise Your Teenagers" during my first charge; these sermons were delivered between the fifth and eleventh birthdays of our oldest one.

This week I heard sad accounts of high school students having parties and drinking beer. Now I have gathered courage to say something about teenagers.

There is one basic mistake most of us parents are inclined to make when our daughter turns fifteen and when our son towers over us at sixteen. We get scared. We aren't afraid that they will beat us up. But we are scared that we might lose them if we lay down the law. There is fear and uncertainty in our hearts when we have to forbid them something—we know they'll demand reasons, and our reasons will not be acceptable to them. That is the moment at which we almost panic. But then we *have* to be parents.

We should never be afraid of our children as long as we love them. And when we take the risk that they are going to hate us, we do it because we love them. As a matter of fact, the moment our daughter shrieks, "I hate you! I hate you!" we know that this has absolutely nothing to do with how much she loves us, as I read somewhere.

Teenagers are extremely uncertain. We parents know this in our hearts; but nobody can tell it by looking at them. They will say, "Don't you trust me?" and instinctively they know they are throwing a curve. It's a tough one to handle. I used to call other parents to ask what time· they had set for the big events their teenagers and ours were attending. Some parents would say, "We trust our John and Jane." But I considered that a cop-out. Trust must be earned. And I often said to our children: "I trust *you*, but I don't trust the devil."

Although we have been disappointed in some parents, we never believed our teenagers when they compared our strictness with "everybody else's parents." There are no parents by that name.

If you love your teenager, you will dare to say no at any risk.

One of the nicest little speeches I ever heard was at a wedding of a nephew of mine. The bridegroom thanked his dad for saying no when God wanted him to say no.

OUTRAGE The seriousness of a crime and a disaster cannot be measured by the reactions of the public.

When 52 hostages were kept in Iran, the Western world was aroused to the verge of war. And the homecoming of the hostages was one of the happiest celebrations. But nobody remembers the names or even the number of the men who died in an unsuccessful attempt to rescue the hostages.

When nearly 80 people drowned in the Potomac River due to an airplane crash, Americans wept at their TV sets. But more than 70 people are killed, not once a year but every day, by soggy, foggy, drunken drivers. There is no public outcry and the carnage continues.

Well, there is some hope: When a drunkard who had been convicted twice for drunken driving and who was out on bail after a third arrest hit and killed Cari Lightner, her mother started the organization Mothers Against Drunk Drivers (MADD). Her campaign has now led to a tough new law in California. Good for her. She may turn around the whole country's lazy attitude. The President of the USA, also a Californian, is going to "create a Commission on Drunk Driving." Which shows what one person can do against the apathy of tens of thousands.

If we want to get rid of people who drive while they are intoxicated, we need not only more frequent drivers' checks and stiffer penalties. The whole attitude of the public must be changed. We need a general agreement that drunks who drive are criminals. It will be hard to instill that conviction. For many years intoxicated drivers got slapped over the wrists with a feather. People are accustomed to thinking that drunks are funny and that racing a car is a joke. Now they should learn that driving while intoxicated is a vicious assault on the safety of innocent people. Especially Christians ought to have their values cleared: we must regard drunks as less hilarious than racial jokes. And we ought to recognize that an intoxicated driver shows as little respect for humanity as a porno-film producer.

Few matters that are worthy of public outrage receive what they deserve.

TO UPHOLD AND TO GOVERN

Recently my wife and I spent an evening and a night in the heart of Chicago. We like to do that, from time to time, in a big city. Nearly all we do is look.

When we drove into the city about 5:00 P.M., I was thinking how close to chaos our metropolitan centers are. But the next morning I was again surprised that they keep running as well as they do.

Just as God's providence continues to uphold and govern the world and all people, so police officers and maintenance crews work twenty-four hours every day to keep big cities going. And just as God's providential works are mostly invisible, so the forces that keep the clock ticking in the inner city have low visibility.

Late at night we found a stairway in the middle of the city. When we descended, we hit upon a whole nether world of concrete and neon lights. Garbage was being carted away; now we knew why the city had not yet choked on its own waste. Supplies were driven in; now we knew how fresh eggs and fresh linens arrive in this wilderness every new morning. And an army of helmeted people worked with noisy equipment, fixing waterlines, reinforcing walls, and digging deeper tunnels.

The life of the city has levels of existence. A surface glance cannot tell what keeps it going. So it is with human life. It consists of much more than biological functions. It has dark tunnels, and windows to eternal lights. But many people never see the whole picture.

There is still law and order in the city. Yes, I know about crime. And many of us have read, seen, or even experienced the lawlessness in cities. Yet it is amazing that red lights make all sinners stop and that they go when they get the green light. People still apologize when they bump against each other on a crowded street. And a young man helped a person in a wheelchair scale the curb of a sidewalk.

I had one moment of near panic: what seemed to be an innumerable host of automobiles was aiming for a narrow street that could only accommodate a trickle at a time. The flow of traffic came from two directions, each driver trying to cut in faster than his or her competitor.

But when my car finally came to the intersection, I saw a policewoman upholding law and order. She had a whistle. She was not young. She stood quite sturdily in the midst of these growling metal beasts. And she looked as reassuring as your mother.

The spectacle so impressed me that my wife had to poke me in the ribs, for the police officer was telling me to round the corner.

NO GREETING TIME

The African people spend much time greeting each other. "Good morning." "Did you sleep well?" "Thanks be to Allah." "How is the work?" "How is the family?" They do it in numerous dialects and in every tribe. Actually the words have been used so often that they have little meaning. The responses are mainly grunts and sounds. But every decent person goes through the elaborate ritual of greeting his or her neighbor. If one does not greet, one is a bad person.

Handshakes are also an art and a ritual. Among the Kuranko you shake with the right hand, and with the left you touch the right forearm of the person you greet. Actually one doesn't press hands; one merely touches. A firm handshake is too assertive and threatening.

The Mende shake hands and follow up with a motion to the heart —as President Reagan and US schoolchildren do when they pledge allegiance to the flag.

The Bassa in Liberia shake your hand firmly, then they fumble for your middle finger and click it with their middle finger. They are completely serious about this business. African Christians have an addi-

tional trick. They first shake hands with the fingers down, the way we do it; then, with the thumb as a hinge, the fingers go up for another shake and finally they go for the middle finger and the click. I shook dozens of hands after a church service. But there weren't many clicks because the fingers were sweaty.

Also among those who speak Hausa, the handshake is followed through by touching the heart.

Until now I had never quite understood that passage in the Bible where Jesus says that his disciples should greet no one on the way (Luke 10:4). Of course I knew it had something to do with the urgency of the message. But I thought that forbidding the messengers to say "hi" and "bye," which is the sum total of the North American ceremony, was carrying things a little far. However, when I saw how a ten-minute walk through the village can easily take an hour because of the required greetings, I understood why the Lord said, "Salute no one on the road." The messenger who is on an errand that makes the difference between life and death has a right to be discourteous.

97

CAMPING   For years our family used to go camping in a large tent we stuffed in the trunk of the car. First we had a big orange tent; then we had a blue one. At one time we even had a special screened-in kitchen tent to go with the ordinary one.

But the children have grown up, and the tents are gone.

This year when the sun got warm and a store had a tent sale, my wife and I bought another tent. It's called a "Family Tent for Four Persons." That means it's adequate for two. Three could sleep in it. But if four persons would crowd in, they would have to leave their toothbrushes outside.

We went for a one-night trial run in a state park on Lake Michigan just north of Muskegon, Michigan. We used to go there eight or ten years ago. At that time our kids climbed up and ran down the dunes that separate the camp from the lake. Now the dunes are off limits; fences and warning signs have been erected. You can't blame the managers. The lake has come up and the dunes are going down.

It was a bit of a nostalgic trip for us. We kept saying: "That's the spot where we set up camp." "That's where I spent a day cutting up a dead tree with a camp saw and a hatchet." "It's a wonder our kids didn't break their limbs when they ran down those dunes."

We liked it so much that we plan to go again. Although I had been told that campers in the state park are now very rowdy, drinking much liquor and making noise late at night, it was not so while we were there. My previous convictions were confirmed—campers are usually nice and ordinary people. They are average citizens with little children and sunburns. In every camp is also the fat man in the big trailer who walks a tiny dog on a long leash early in the morning and late at night. You always find a couple who have a portable TV on a picnic table. Next to us were five boys in one tent. But they had their radios in headsets, permanently glued to their ears. And they closed the day with a dance around their fire while they waved sparklers, left over from the Fourth of July. My wife and I thought they were well behaved.

We walked the beach of Lake Michigan and came to a spot where a colony of swallows had their nests bored in the hard sand of the bank. The whole sandy wall looked like a swiss cheese. When we kept still for a while, we could hear the concert of the young swallows in the nests. And the parents would fly forth and back bringing food to their young. Each bird knew its own nest in that honeycombed wall. And there must have been two hundred little holes.

This summer we'll go camping again. Not for weeks, just now and then for a night or two. In the evening I will tend to a little fire with great care. And when we crawl into our sleeping bags, we will think that we are rich and that life is simple.

Married people must talk to each other. As the experts say, the "partners must learn to communicate." Communication is more than conversation.

At the Cedar Lake Bible Conference, where I gave speeches this summer, was a young couple with two red-haired kids. My wife has red-heads in her family and was always hoping that we would have a child with red hair. It did not work.

Well, these lucky parents of the auburn-haired put their young children to bed every day after lunch. Then they would sit across from each other in lawn chairs under a big tree. Each would hold a bottle of pop ("soda," they say in Sheboygan) and they would talk lazily for an hour to an hour and a half. Every so often he or she would get up to listen at the screen of the children's bedroom. Then they would continue to sit there, simply enjoying each other's company.

If they are reading this page, I assure this couple that I was not eavesdropping. My window was closed, and I was working on the evening's speech. The little air conditioner was going full blast in my room.

I did get sentimental about the loving way this couple sat across from each other.

Now I advise every couple, and especially those who are having marital problems, to place two chairs across from each other, just as the parents of the red-haired children did. Sit in these chairs for one hour to one hour and a half each day for a full week. Each may have one bottle of pop (or "soda," as they say in Wisconsin). Then look at each other. Smile at each other. Talk to each other. Repeat this exercise until you have learned to communicate.

WINDOWS IN HEAVEN

About forty years ago I felt the vise of hunger in my stomach. Today I cannot quite remember it.

My mother still managed to prepare food, three times a day. But there was no such thing as a solid meal. After we had eaten, we wanted to eat again. But we had to wait for five hours.

"Go to bed early," she used to say, "then you don't think about your stomach."

Sometimes it comes back to me. I saw a commercial on TV where food is advertised because it does not feed. "I love the way it looks on me," the woman sings. That is a very immoral song.

We had thought the war would have been over. But here it was April 1945, and the Germans were still hanging on. In the western part of Holland, where I lived, the Nazis were shooting a new weapon at Great Britain. It was the V-2, the forerunner of all of today's missiles.

Our neighbor was talking with my father. Both men agreed that Germany would lose the war. But the neighbor said that freedom would come too late. "Most people in the city will starve to death."

"We must pray," said my father. He always said that. "Prayer is the mightiest weapon," he proclaimed. And one of the German V-2s whistled overhead.

"Don't expect miracles," said our neighbor. "Thousands of people are going to die before summer; and you know it."

"But God can make windows in heaven," said Dad. He raised his voice. He always did that when he confessed his faith. It seemed as if his heart was trying to outshout his head.

Like the captain in Samaria (2 Kings 7:2), our neighbor did not deny God's omnipotence. He merely shrugged his shoulders.

Then came the end of April and the first days of May. Rumors were rife. We were told that Hitler was dead and that the German army had collapsed. We lived between hope and fear, tops of joy, pits of despair. And the gun-toting Germans were still in the street.

It was on one of these days that we saw the most beautiful sight the eyes of hungry people have ever seen. Low-flying British and

American bombers and transport planes flew overhead. The bomb-doors opened and they dropped containers with food in the pasture. A whirlwind of leaflets fluttered over the town. The leaflets were in German: This is a mercy mission for the Dutch population; don't interfere!

My father's eyes were moist when he looked at the planes. And he did not raise his voice when he said, "God has opened the windows of heaven."

HEATWAVE   At the time of this writing we are living through a heat wave. My base-ment is not so bad, but when I come upstairs it feels as if I am swallow-ing a wet rag. We had a few short and heavy thunderstorms, but they did not bring down the temperature. Everybody tells everybody that it's hot and muggy.

The discomfort of extreme heat is well known. Almost 200 years ago the British novelist Jane Austen had a "dreadfully hot" summer and complained to her sister Cassandra: "I am in a continuous state of inelegance." I think she was worried that her skirt got wrinkled.

Very few of us attempt to keep up a dignified appearance during a heat wave. It's fun to look at the hundreds of people who escape to air-conditioned malls and supermarkets. The young and lean don't look so bad in skimpy clothing. But most older folks look positively inelegant, as Austen would say. I went with my wife to the supermarket rather late one evening, and I saw a retired Calvin College professor in the store. Ordinarily I would have chatted with him, but I merely waved from behind a shelf of cans and cookies because I had just become conscious of my "inelegance."

When I was young, I was taught that people in hot countries have loose morals. And in countries where people have to wear overcoats for eight out of twelve months (and raincoats for the rest of the year), they are more upright.

It's one of those myths, of course. The people I saw in West and South Africa were dignified, and they used clothing to enhance their dignity. That's why one sees more bare flesh in our churches on Sunday during a heat wave than in a Nigerian church.

As for moral laxness, at this moment it seems to me that during periods of very oppressive heat, people lack the energy for any strenuous work, be it good or evil.

Emotionally we are all affected by the heat. When the whole family is hot and bothered, it's easy to get into a scrap. And we have often been told that "long hot summers" contribute to riots.

Extreme heat is no blessing. It's probably a curse. One of the benefits enjoyed by the saved multitude in Revelation 7 is that "the sun shall not strike them nor any scorching heat." But as long as we are this side of the sea of crystal, we are required to retain some sort of elegance in all circumstances.

Funny, isn't it? that as soon as we are two weeks into winter we won't be able to imagine this heat anymore. We'll merely remember the pleasant warmth of the summer.

LIVING WITH PAIN

Once I was reading Scripture to a man who was in the hospital because he had kidney stones. He got an attack just when I was at verse 7 of Hebrews 12. He doubled up in agony and said, "Oh god, oh god, oh god." I don't know if he was swearing or praying. He certainly did not listen to the Bible reading.

People who suffer intense pain cannot think of anything else. Pain overpowers people. They cannot listen to Beethoven or the Bible. Their whole being burns with pain.

Sorrow is the pain of the spirit. Intense grief does the same thing as physical pain: it overwhelms or fills a person. When sorrow has overwhelmed a person, all the goodness in the world cannot enter his or her door.

Not all pain is so intense that it overwhelms us. All of us have areas in our lives that are hurting. But we can still laugh.

It helps our growth in unity to remember that we are all hurting. I often look around at a roomful or a churchful of people and say to myself, Everyone has a pain, everyone needs comfort. Such a thought dispels envy and carries compassion to the soul.

Healthy people control their pain. They keep their sorrow in a corner of their lives. But some people are too tired or too weak to keep the hurt in a limited place. Then the mental pain makes a prisoner of those people. Sorrow may become such a familiar tyrant that the victim lacks the ambition to shake loose.

Sooner or later all of us must learn how to live with sorrow. We may not hide it too deeply; it will explode. We may not cherish it too much; it will dominate.

At night our spirits are usually weak. When I wake up during the night, I always think of something unpleasant. My little pain becomes a big sorrow and I cannot escape its grip. I don't wake up very often, and I seldom cry. But when I wake up with pain, nothing else will enter the door of my life.

I have a little remedy, and I suppose most of you do. I get up and have tea and crackers. I read and I pray. Most of the time my tyrant lets go. But sometimes it takes a long time.

"Weeping may tarry for the night, but joy comes with the morning" (Ps. 30:5). The night may be long, but God lets none of his children suffer forever.

ARGUE, YOU LOSE An elderly friend of mine used to say that a person cannot argue with the devil. He was right. We are lost as soon as we argue. The minute we show interest in the devil's proposals we have sinned. Our argument is merely an attempt to reduce the damage—as if it were ever calculable.

Eve should have said: "No, get out!"

Samson should never have dallied with Delilah.

Aaron should have said: "Golden calf? Over my dead body!"

"Resist the devil, and he will flee from you," says James. But as soon as you give him a come-on, you are lost. When you say, "Let's discuss that," you are halfway across the bridge.

But how do you know that the devil is making a proposal? Isn't it so that most suggestions don't seem to come directly from God or the devil?

Be careful now. Eve, Samson, and Aaron should have been able to see the devil behind the suggestion. And you and I must not make our ethical decisions more difficult than they need to be. Let's keep the art of living as simple as possible. We simplify it considerably by admitting that there are lots of suggestions that should never be considered and there are plenty of proposals that deserve a no without second thoughts. If she is the neighbor's wife and if it is the company's money, the answer is no. Expressions such as "but I love her so much" and "I need it so much" are the whining sounds of someone who thought he could argue with the devil.

Of course, not all decisions are simple. You and I have heard a thousand times that life is difficult and our world is complex. You have also noticed, perhaps, that people emphasize the difficulty of living and the complexity of our world when they want to justify shady practices and shady living. In their world it's neither light nor dark. They cannot say yes and they cannot say no. Their whole world is one feeble "maybe."

The Bible says that we should be "wise as to what is good and guileless as to what is evil" (Rom. 16: 19). But in most high school classes and TV shows the admiration goes to those who are insiders in the realm of evil, while they are underdeveloped in the art of doing good.

All of us will find it a lot easier to say no to the devil when we make it a practice to say yes to God.

I am writing this in praise of routine. One might expect such a piece from a person who has been away from his work for a long time. But even professional wanderers cannot enjoy life without a regular rhythm, I think. These vagabonds will boast that they do not sleep two nights in the same bed. However they don't tell us that they always sleep on their right side and never on their back. They hate to admit they're in a rut.

If life without rules were possible, it would certainly be boring. It would be like music without rhythm and worship without liturgy; it would have neither pep nor point.

The youth of Western Europe, we thought, had broken all the rules to live a wild and woolly life. Now it is reported that Protestant kids in France and in Holland are falling in love with monasteries. I have never lived in a monastery, but I know of retreats where a rigid discipline is imposed. There's something very comforting about seasons and rules decreed by higher orders for our well-being. The reliable rhythms of rising, praying, eating, and working by the sound of the bell is like a sturdy embrace that gives security to the drifter.

Muslims have a rhythm in their religious living that can make us envious. I have seen them in mosques, markets, and airports. They pray when it's time to pray.

Our ancestors prayed at the sight of food on the table. I still do that. But I hear of many who don't. Many Christians are admitting that they should pray more and, perhaps, sing more, but they don't know how to manage their time. Some say that a call to prayer and worship twice a week is one too many. It infringes on their freedom.

And we *are* free, of course. But just as nearly every one of us needs an alarm clock to get out of bed and a punch clock to get to work on time, so we need a bell to call us to prayer and a siren that indicates that we should pause for a doxology.

We need a spiritual routine to get us out of a bad rut. Ultimately it is a choice between one routine or another.

TOTAL DEPRAVITY

Permit me to talk once again about the war. I want to show why I cannot stand Christian Reformed people making in-house jokes about total depravity.

In the little town of my youth the owners of the butchershop were Jewish. They were the first ones to feel the claws of the Nazi beast during the German occupation. I remember seeing the butcher's son, who was about my age, with a yellow star on his jacket. It said that he was a *Jude*, a Jew. I was embarrassed when I met him. So were most of my friends. But others were uncertain. Maybe Jews were dangerous.

Then all the Jews were ordered to leave town and go to a center in Germany. My father and my uncle seemed to know much more about German intentions than most people did. My uncle went to talk to the butcher's family. "You must hide," my uncle said. "The Germans are going to kill you; I'll help you find a place to hide." But Gabe said, "No; that would give you a lot of trouble, and I don't think it will be as bad as all that."

I can still see the family board the bus. They wore their yellow stars, and there were a few German soldiers on the bus.

The whole family was killed. We never learned where and how.

When the war was over, my pals and I emerged with the underground forces. I had a light automatic gun and guarded Nazi prisoners. One night when we learned that one of our friends had been tortured and killed during the war, we lined up our prisoners and were going to give them some of their own medicine. But a carpenter of our town, who was also the organist in our church, said, "You will touch them only over my dead body." That brought us to our Christian senses.

Total depravity is the only accurate and biblical way of describing humanity outside of Christ. I know it deep in my heart. We are all capable of all possible crimes and incapable of any real improvement outside of the grace of God. I have no trust whatsoever in culture and civilization. All the paint will wash off in one little flood.

Some Christians are so feeble in their statements about our need for regeneration. And some preachers are so broadminded in ascribing goodness to many human endeavors. It's not only that they read their Bibles poorly; they have never looked into the eyes of the devil.

WHY?   The difficult question little children ask is, Why?

They ask it about the habits of animals and people. They want to know why roses have thorns and why only ministers may drink water in church.

Interrogation by a child four to six years old can be grueling for an adult. The most recent such questioning I have witnessed occurred in an airplane; a mother was traveling with two of these inquisitors. A be-jeweled woman on the same airplane carried a mini-dog that wore a little coat and was provided with a little padded house. She had to answer many questions. But the most direct attack was on a muscleman who had a big blue and red tattoo on his arm. "What's that?" "A tattoo." "How did you make it?" "With a needle." And then came the question for the rationale: "Why?" The man was poked by his friends and giggled about by others, but he never came up with an answer that could satisfy the children and turn the bright eyes to another object.

Teenagers do not ask, Why? Their difficult question is, Why not?

Their area of inquiry is mainly permissible behavior.

Shall I buy a new outfit, visit a friend, go to the party, see the show, stay up late, stay out long?

If the question where, Why? one would need a good reason for do-ing these things. Since the question is, Why not? someone has to prove that great harm will come from doing what is being proposed.

Adults do not ask, Why? or, Why not? Their difficult question is, So what? They have accepted the world as it comes: Roses are red and violets are blue. So what? Some people carry mini-dogs on airplanes and others have tattoos all over their arms. So what? Adults have made their decisions. They have married, they have received money, and they have spent money. They have done what they have done for whatever reason. So what?

So what? is the self-defense of the committed. Maybe they married the wrong spouse and perhaps they did get off the right track somewhere along the line. They don't ask, Why? and it is too late for, Why not? The only challenge the adult can hurl at others who may be thinking, It's wrong, it's stupid, it's sin, is, So what?

Until we become children once again. Then we wonder why things are the way they are. And we analyze the complex motivations of the human heart that triggered our actions. Once again we dare ask, Why?

PAST TENSE IS FOREVER

This is the first September in twenty-four years that we have no children to send off to school.

We have a picture of our oldest child being accompanied by her mother to the first day in grade one, and we have a picture of our youngest one graduating from high school. That's it. That spans two dozen years of buying back-to-school clothing, paying tuition, attending parent-teacher meetings, reading report cards, writing excuses for illness or "due to family circumstances she cannot attend...," et cetera. It's all past.

These years comprise countless stories about teachers who were nice, who were mean, who talked too much, who were "neat" and "cool" and, sometimes, "real Christians." Teachers got to know our children the way we hardly knew them, but our children also got to know their teachers the way they hardly know themselves. Now it's history.

We have attended track meets, ball games, spelling bees, school events, plays, bazaars, concerts, and commencement exercises. Sometimes one of our children passed from one grade to another by the mercy of the teachers, and some of our offspring have given valedictory speeches at graduation time. All I remember is how warm it was and how well dressed they were.

Some of our (six) children took tests and grades too seriously, and some did not take them seriously enough. To the one we had to say, "Time to do your homework," and to the other, "Time to quit and go to bed." And now that time is past.

We have waited up for the children to return from school parties. In fact, I don't think I have ever gone to bed before the children were home, as long as they were of high school age. We have said, more than twenty-four times, that the summer vacations were too long but always, and before we knew it, it would be September. And this September, the first in twenty-four years, we have no children to get ready for school. It's irrevocably past.

We were not model parents, as many know, and our children were not model children, as numerous people know. But there it is; it's finished. We have gone through countless little joys and little sorrows. We have paid a pile of Christian school tuition, and we have prayed for students and teachers every school day for twenty-four years.

Now I'm not posing as an expert, I'm merely saying to parents with school-going children: Give it your best shot; you don't get a second chance.

THE FINAL ANSWER

Dr. Richard S. Wierenga, a retired dentist, was deeply interested in the eternal destiny of human beings who died in infancy. For years he studied the Bible, quizzed theologians, and read whatever might help him arrive at a conclusion. Finally he wrote an essay, "Heaven—the Cathedral of Eternity." But by the time it appeared in print, Wierenga himself was moving from the narthex to the cathedral, using his own terms. He died last week.

Letters are still coming to the office saying "Wierenga is right" and "Wierenga is wrong," and I keep thinking that, by now, Wierenga has probably counted all the babies in heaven.

It is an awesome thought that dying people are in the hands of God's angels the minute they slip out of our embrace. I can think of a number of people whose pastor and counselor I was until the moment they passed through the curtain. Then I would look at the lifeless body and think: Now you know it much better than I.

Most people have a list of questions they would like to present to God. We would like to ask him about babies in heaven and about women in office. I have some exegetical questions: What's that line about people being baptized for the dead (1 Cor. 15:29), and what did you mean in 1 Peter 3:19, about Christ preaching to spirits in prison?

Sometimes, when we get stuck in a conversation about "unanswered" prayers or God's sovereignty and our responsibility, someone says, "We'll know the answer hereafter."

I am not so sure that we'll get our answers in heaven. We may have lost our list of questions by that time.

I think our arrival in heaven will be more like this: When I was a young man, I was separated from my fiancée for a whole year with a whole ocean between us. Correspondence is indispensable but unfulfilling during such a time. Little questions become big problems. Minor uncertainties become raging suspicions. When I finally traveled to her, I had a long list of matters that needed to be cleared up, urgently! But at the moment of meeting, all of it melted away. With the first touch, the importance of the questions became zero, for the presence was overwhelming.

Someday everything will become lucid. But it won't be because God is going to answer our list of questions. His Presence will be overwhelming. And all our weary questions will dissipate when we are kissed by God.

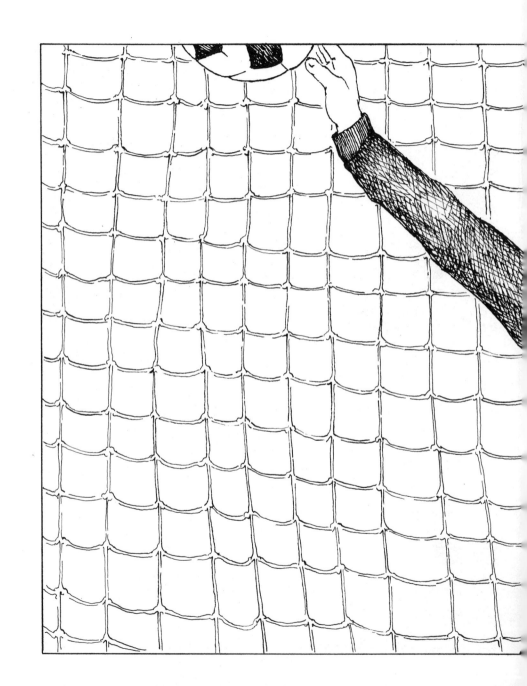